16$\frac{00}{}$

VIEW FROM A MISSISSIPPI RIVER COTTON SACK

SECOND EDITION

WRITTEN AND ILLUSTRATED
BY
FRANCES BRINKLEY COWDEN

EDITED BY
MARCELLE B. ZARSHENAS

GRANDMOTHER EARTH CREATIONS
GERMANTOWN, TENNESSEE

View From a Mississippi River Cotton Sack
COPYRIGHT © 1993 by Frances Cowden
and *GRANDMOTHER EARTH CREATIONS*
ALL RIGHTS RESERVED

Library of Congress Catalog Card Number:
93-080265

ISBN 1-884289-03-7 21.95

GRANDMOTHER EARTH CREATIONS
8463 DEERFIELD LANE
GERMANTOWN, TENNESSEE 38138

FIRST PRINTING: PEERLESS PRINTING, AUGUST, 1993
LIBRARY EDITION: PEERLESS PRINTING, JANUARY, 1994

This book is dedicated to my family. May the memory of those who have gone before us be kept alive in the hearts of those who come afterwards. May we all remember the importance of the gifts of beauty and love that God has given us to preserve and share.

GRANDMOTHER EARTH CREATIONS
prints all books on recycled paper
in accordance with their philosophy of helping to preserve the earth.
For the same reason most of the customary blank pages are omitted.

ACKNOWLEDGMENTS:

Work from this collection have appeared in the following publications:

AMBER (CANADA)
THE COMMERCIAL APPEAL
CONTEMPORARY POETS OF ARKANSAS
ETCHINGS ACROSS THE MOON (By Frances Brinkley)
MID-SOUTH POETRY CONSORTIUM
OF BUTTERFLIES AND UNICORNS
(By Eve Braden Hatchett and Frances Brinkley Cowden)
SOUTH AND WEST
TENNESSEE VOICES
VOICES INTERNATIONAL

Special thanks to the following people:

Sue Abbott Boyd, Fort Smith, Arkansas, who sponsored *VOICES INTERNATIONAL* for the three years that I was editor, published my first book *ETCHING ACROSS THE MOON* and poems I wrote during my early years in *SOUTH AND WEST.*

Lourine White, Piggott, Arkansas, who introduced me to the world of poets and learning to write, helped me with *VOICES INTERNATIONAL,* and let me help her with *"The Poetry Dial,"* a column in *THE PIGGOTT BANNER.*

Clovita Rice, Little Rock, Arkansas, editor of *VOICES INTERNATIONAL,* for encouragement and support for twenty-five years.

Juanita B. Harris, Osceola , Arkansas, who taught me the true meaning of being an artist and encouraged me to study visual art.

Eve Braden Hatchett, Memphis, Tennessee, who challenged me to continue my poetry during the years I have been in Memphis.

Marcelle Brinkley Zarshenas, Germantown, Tennessee--my daughter and editor.

Ruth Owen, Memphis, Tennessee, for years of proof-reading my work.

Members of The Poetry Society of Tennessee for their support.

CONTENTS

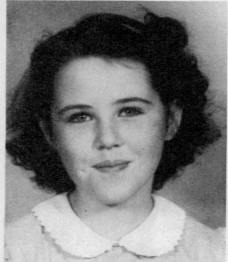

Frances Tacker in the second grade at Whitton Elementary

*A*n artist and potter as well as a poet, Frances Cowden has taken the fiber and liquid of experience and imagination and molded them into memorable poems in *VIEW FROM A MISSISSIPPI RIVER COTTON SACK.*

Autobiographical, the poems reminisce, all the way from early childhood mud pies to herself as a grandmother. She recalls picking cotton "like pulling dreams from cotton candy," and waiting for her father to come home after marketing his cotton "with pockets full of the world." And she describes the more recent experience of taking her grandmother to a circus where the roles of child and adult are now reversed.

Multiple legacies abound in the poems, including strong family values, love of the land and the river, and the magnetic pull of the dreamer, of giving "in to the magic" and forgiving "the dark claws."

Appealing to the various senses, this collection is rich with imagery. A sunset "sizzles on the edge of her mind/like one more fritter/on the cast iron skillet." And she took "secrets whispered only to me/put them into poems/sailing them/like the cottonwood seeds/on a windy summer afternoon." Though in one poem she was describing her mother as a tall woman whose shadow was taller, one senses that Frances herself not only has grown taller in physical stature, but that her shadow has matured from the child dreaming on the cotton sack to the grandmother now teaching her grandchildren to mold clay and words. . .

And when her "poems are spoken/there are still enough words/left to drift to the sea promising drama for generation after generation of poets/and river dreamers.

Clovita Rice, editor,
VOICES INTERNATIONAL

MISSISSIPPI RIVER LEGACY

Into the blade-sparkling waters
I cast my river dreams
back to
long before my fathers came
long before the first Indian
stooped to drink--
always there was the power
of the river ...

As a child I crossed the
bridge from Arkansas to Memphis
in awe
of mysterious currents
whispering tales of
drownings and other disasters--

Thousands of tongues have sought
to paint its ever-changing
un-changing mystery--
yet the same tranquil waters
darkened by murder
suicides
and twists of fate

nourish the fisherman's hook
     and excite the boatman.
The poet looks for illusive words
throwing in his hook and waiting---
when his poems are spoken
    there are still enough words
    left to drift
      with the wind to the sea
promising drama
for generation after generation
    of poets
    and river dreamers.

SOMETHING FROM WITHIN

It came to me while lying
on the back porch
looking up at miraculous stars
remembering
how Grandma talked of pearly gates and golden slippers.
I do not remember the clothes she wore--
they were not fashionable-fancy
but either hand-sewn
or bought at Tyronza Supply.
She used to make us cookies and pump us water...
Standing there with that fresh, cool elixir--
magic though without ice from the ice-box,
"Not Solomon in all his glory"
could have made a more beautiful image.
Drinking from the same dipper,
we ran to play in the sun.
She didn't need
golden slippers...
perhaps the stars told me
perhaps it was something from within.

MONKEY SHOW

Wheelchair bound
playing hooky from the nursing home
with two fifty year-old teenagers...
who brought Grandma
to the zoo during spring break,
Grandma laughed at the monkeys--
watched nimble bodies cavort and scream
like junior high kids let out of an English class
into a gym.
Not even her great-great-grandchild in the stroller
out-laughed Grandma,
not even the visiting day-care gang had more fun.
Grandma laughed at the monkeys
jumping rope between yesterday and tomorrow
wedging rainbow memories
into a private prism
to dance across a gray wall
on rainy April days.
Later that summer
when Grandma died,
one granddaughter said to the other,
"She thinks that trip to the zoo was just for her."
"I know," the other one said.

VIEW FROM A MISSISSIPPI RIVER COTTON SACK

She was one of the children who walked the cotton patch
from spring until fall
stooped with a sharp blade segregating weeds
from cotton stalks from sunrise until sundown
until the summer was almost gone...
praying for shade daring to hope for rain.
In September she came home from school
to harvest the white gold that stole her Saturday leisure
and made her curl up inside herself
like the soft balls wanting to be released from dark claws.
Unlike the children of the sharecroppers
she could escape to school
while they slaved on until the tyrant crop was gone.
Her parents loved her but they too had been
children of the poor and didn't know any other way.
She was slower than the rest,
she would pick just enough cotton to make a comfortable bed
then lie down hidden within the foliage
and find pleasure in the sound of dry leaves crushing
and in releasing the soft white fiber
like pulling dreams from cotton candy.
Younger Bobby and Janice always weighed in more
when it was time to go...
during the ride home nestled in soft cotton piled high
the warm smell of harvested clouds,
she gave in to the magic and forgave the dark claws.

12

THE OLDER I GET THE TALLER MY MOTHER BECOMES

She must have known a thousand songs
and
she
sang
them
all
to
us...
she made us forget when we were hungry
or
didn't
have
a
pretty
dress...
She was a tall woman and her shadow
was
taller
keeping
us
safe
even
as
we grew
older.

13

OF SWORDS AND PLOWSHARES

for my father
and for President Bill Clinton

Instead of bullets into flesh
he planted seeds in fertile Delta soil
plotting strategy against the weather. . .
when he
with his family of small children
was deferred from the draft. . .
his battle was
to multiply upon the earth
instead of dividing--
his will
keen steel
a match for any plow or sword.

His children and his children's children
can testify
you do not have to shoulder bayonets
or ride rockets
to have
what it really takes.

A REMEMBRANCE FOR PETE: MY GRANDDAD

Sun-toned
taught by earth and rain--
a farm boy
he went to Paris a Doughboy
but came back to the soil
to rear his family on laughter and love
throughout depression, drought and storm.

When I was six
he was the tallest man alive
and carried me on his shoulders
across flooded fields or through the snow to school.
Patient--
and as silent as the "blue-eyed" catfish
he caught for me--
he listened while I dreamed.

When I heard he had died,
I ate the last okra and tomatoes from his garden
went outside by the willow tree
and sat until morning--

Twenty years and my own grandchildren later
I still cannot say goodbye.

15

VALENTINE QUEEN

Ninety years young
with a hundred grandchildren
counting greats and great-greats--
she stepped up to receive her crown
at the nursing home gala
asking, "Why me?"
Forty-odd years ago
she was a cook in Whitton Elementary cafeteria
and we shared our grandmother
with the whole school.
"Susie, now you know those peas are good for you."
"Victoria, honey, you are never
going to get any meat on those bones
if you don't drink your milk."
The Minor boys ate all the beans they could hold.
At the Methodist Church we sang
"Bringing in the Sheaves"
and I always thought of Grandma,
even when I thought it meant bringing in the sheets.
My best friends always tried to steal my grandma--
she offered a cup of friendship to everyone she met.
She lived her last days in the tiny
half-room of the nursing home
cheering others in every way she could.
They voted her queen, but she earned her title
in our eyes long ago:
Grandma Gladys, Queen of Hearts.

LEGENDS UNWRITTEN

...a portrait in the attic---
a family of familiar eyes--my father's. . . .
My grandfather sat, a baby,
with ten brothers and sisters staring forward.
The young wife was the great-grandmother
I once knew as an old woman with white hair
who lay in the bed waiting for my childhood kisses.
She sat by her Indian mother in braids and beads --
now I know why earth and sky hold magic. . .
The husband, my great grandfather, glared out with eyes hiding
stories that would never be told.
"Throw that picture away!" my father told me.
"You would think he had been hanged as a horse thief..."
my mother whispered.
"The handsome man with strange eyes..."
Wild horses
deep rivers
and legends unwritten
raced through my mind.

HER FACE

Sometimes I see her face
wizened and brown as the knob
of the bed post of her cheap and scarred bed.
The tiny woman, gnarled like the cotton bolls
she grubbed for
after the main crop was harvested,
lived on snuff and chocolate gravy
and had a tall grisly husband
that I wish I could paint
and call "The Sharecropper."
An older daughter always
wore her hair in curlers
and giggled
at the rolling store man
they stopped for baloney,
R. C.'s and candy
for the two-year old
still nursed by Mamma--
but the artist son had blue eyes
and the smile of a gypsy--
I would have married him
had I been older than twelve
when they moved on.

FROM INSIDE THE SKILLET

Dust settles as the Delta sunset rolls across the plowed fields
and crinkles of dark trees that line the edge of
Dead Timber Lake.
Facing westward toward the crimson fog
she watches as black engulfs the last
fire coal of day --
one settling of life less
though tomorrow's repeat performance
sizzles on the edge of her mind
like one more fritter
on the cast iron skillet.
From inside the windows blaze orange
and nightly chores wait like
a red-hot oven unappeased no matter how much wood
is shoved into its ruby mouth.
She walks to the edge of the porch
almost tripping over the Irish setter
glued to the steps--
Rudy is always in the way.
A toddler in a scarlet shirt
waddles through the door waving a spoon.
She picks him up -- then his britches
and walks slowly toward the swing.
Singing softly hugging him to her breast
they swing like crickets
waiting for the moon.

19

COTTONWOOD SECRETS

Visions of my other sister
lie deep within my soul's mirror--
a cottonwood with sun-splashed dancing leaves
linked to another tree by a log
my father placed there so he could hang
two tire swings for six lively children and their playmates.
I could sit in one of the swings for stolen hours
and watch red or green tractors,
harvesters or cars go by on the gravel road.
I could climb up into my tree sister's arms
and watch Janice and Bobby or Cletus Jr.
fishing for crawdads
in the ditch down the road.
I exchanged my deepest dreams with her--
I would never tell Linda or Janice or Nancy.
My tree sister never told anyone my secrets...
But I took the secrets whispered only to me
put them into poems
sailing them
like the cottonwood seeds
on a windy summer afternoon.

SERAPHENIA

Shade-starved she lay
on yielding grass
painting cloud pictures
fantasy after fantasy --
the cottonwood tree defined
the secret
but she was not ready to listen.

Sweat-bathed she pulled off
the soaked shirt and fanned herself
with her wet straw hat.
Soon they would be coming for her -
noisy / clanky / with sharp hoes.
No matter--
they could not fire anyone
not getting paid.

She closed her eyes
praying for night to come
and erase the sun.

21

MUD-PIE LEGACY

After each summer rain
mud pies lined my childhood window sill.
Janice and I taught Nancy and Linda
how to roll little mud balls
and pick dandelions
to garnish our dishes which we fashioned inside fruit jar lids
stolen from mother's preserve-making.
Legends name the earth holy--
something that gives birth
something to die for...
When I walked the plowed earth barefooted
with my father--a farmer--
I learned the ritual of fertility
and wondered how many before me
had the power.
Now I make clay pots
line them up for sale
and wonder if those who buy my vessels
know the meaning within.
I teach my grandchildren to mold and shape
remembering how the native Americans
dug their clay
from the Mississippi
and buried the pots
with their loved ones
returning earth to earth.

COTTON CARNIVAL:
LOOKING BACK FROM MEMPHIS

Leaping from the curb to catch the gold doubloon
tossed by the Cotton Carnival Queen
I was a child again
bouncing wild on white cotton heaped
into the trailer by strong black hands.
I floated on clouds of far away dreams
danced like maidens mashing grapes
buried myself in the warm musk--
when Daddy took it to the gin
it came back oranges, candy, new clothes.
From air crisp as the drying cotton leaves
past the porch strung with onions and peppers
stacked with bushels of sweet potatoes
I would run into a kitchen
warm with pumpkin pie and cracklin' bread.
Now I walk up gray concrete steps
into a hallway dim and grimy
piled high with the children the age I was once --
but I wonder what the ghetto has to offer
at harvest time and why carnival balloons are so high
on this spring day.

CHOCOLATE DREAMS

I had never seen my father really ill
hospital-clad and staked into place
with miles of tubes
conniving---
face red and swollen
unable to talk
unable to eat
unable to sleep
Could this be the man
who came home from
the cotton gin
pockets full of the world. . .
Baby Ruth bars
hidden among flour and potatoes?
There were six children
the earth and his wit
to feed us--
farming
hunting and fishing
peddling auction sale bargains.

Vertical looks better--
after fifty years
I understand
the importance of chocolate candy
and praying
"Now I lay me down to sleep."

A GOLD COIN
for Mother

When the moon is a gold coin on black felt,
I remember how once you made a jack-o-lantern
from a cardboard box and showed us
the witch riding across the moon.
In later years we must have had pumpkin jack-o-lanterns,
but I don't remember them.
The Christmas tree that year was the first one I remember--
a pine limb with tissue paper from oranges and apples
cut in happy tassels.
I remember how you sang and told stories
long before television cartoons.
Now you buy masks and Halloween candy
and decorate a tree piled with gifts for *our children*.
I wonder if the glowing baubles and shiny toys
are more beautiful than a gold coin on black felt.

WAR GAMES

My first memory was of Bobby
breaking my porcelain figurine
Great-Grandma Bullard had brought
over from Germany.
I forgave him because I was almost four
he was only two
mama spanked him
and he cried and called me "Diddy."
But he never got away with another thing--
accident or not.
Bobby and I didn't just fight
we did battle--
we chose sides from among the other brothers and sisters
and wrestled in the grass
until one of the younger ones got hurt and
went running to Mama--
sometimes
Bobby and I did single combat...
almost every day we got into some kind of fight--
despite the inevitable switch.
At the time I thought it was his fault
I got whippings every day--
but when I was in the eighth grade
and he was in the seventh...
I realized that there was no longer a contest--
suddenly the battles stopped
and I was his "diddy" once again.

YOUNGER DREAMS

FOR CLAY, MY ARTIST SON

I push aside the books
bits of thread
old magazines
and other memories
that crowd me from my bed...
Here
closed in by letters
and younger dreams,
I lie alone
yet
not
all alone
as on some wide, wide sea
before the albatross was killed...
I drink from that same cup
as when I crept out of bed as a child
and climbed to the top of the old shed
to wait for the magic
of morning glories
waking with the dew
sunrise
being painted across the Delta
and sounds of summer...
waking up to sizzle.

27

AT THE END OF THE NIGHT

In spite of all she had endured
she clung to life...
memory hopscotched within a pale body
imprisoned between stone-white sheets.
It is time for jumping rope
between pain and death.
Under skin that hung rejecting flesh
--little girl fast asleep--
not even she could see how much she had loved
or what dreams she has wasted
pacing floor after linoleum floor
waiting for her husband
out drinking and spending.
Even when at fifty he found religion
and quit alcohol,
she worried about children and grandchildren
buried her first-born daughter
nursed broken bones
and cracked dreams.
Ten years later
after they buried
my grandfather by her side,
I dreamed I saw her in her old rocking chair
all worry finally erased from her smiling face.
"I'm happy," she glowed.
"My love is with me now."

THE LADY ON THE PORCH

I did not know
when you came to me in the night
the wind blowing through your hair
and the mist caressing my cheek
and the creak of the swing
against the night pulse
how could I know
snow would seep in.
The next day I went back
the sun had pushed back the wind
and the swing did not creak.
I pushed the swing
with timid fingers
and stood there
embracing your shadow.

GRANDMA SINGS EVERY EASTER

I thought I saw her in the crowd--
gray haired, wearing glasses
a smile echoing last Easter
when she really was there...

Other silver-haired grandmothers
looked toward the choir remembering services
when they had not been alone--
trying to keep the clean-faced and crisply-dressed
boys and girls they had brought with them
crisp, and above all, quiet.
For thousands of Easter mornings Grandma had sung
these songs and heard these words.
"Lo, He is not in the tomb."
"Christ the Lord has risen today! "
"Hallelujah! Hallelujah!"
Now I wait to hide colored eggs
with my own grandchildren and feed them ham.
I join the chorus as
tears turn to joy.
Easter is not the time to mourn,
nor is there any reason to.
Grandma is somewhere singing
"Hallelujah! Hallelujah!"

HER GOLDEN THREAD

for Eve and Bill

He slipped away but left a golden thread...
He loved her with a love beyond compare.
He left no deeds nor words of love unsaid--
  The roses that he sent still linger there
        where...around the moon
     and back again
      they climbed
       sifting stars
Into a diamond for each lonely night
She had to live without his eager touch.
A part of him is sewn within her soul...
  He slipped away but left a golden thread.

BALLOONS FOR EMILY

Emily was only four when the sky caved in--
we prayed but were afraid--
remembering pale-eyed Leonard
who died of leukemia
when we were in the fourth grade.
The treatments made her sick
and all of her amber curls melted away;
her once-bright eyes cried
when we drove anywhere near St. Jude...
Yet those angels in white coats without wings
but with invisible wands
(given by the dollars and dimes
from people we would never meet)
were the only angels Emily was to meet just yet.
The Make-A-Wish Foundation
sent her to Disney World,
but our wish came true
when she came running into the house
beautiful; new curls flying in the wind
clutching her balloons from a St. Jude party
smiling like the sun
on a cloudless new sky.

32

JUST TURTLES

What can you do with a kid like that
trying to write poetry
about a row of turtles lined up on a log?
But the swamp is full of logs
crowded with lazy reptiles
just sitting there drinking the sun;
there ought to be a better market
for turtles
then we could sell them
every Sunday morning.

LEMONADE

I sat another Sunday afternoon
drawing on the cold misty glass
wondering why I bothered.
I pulled out the straw
and taking the glass in both hands
drank
making love
with my tongue
with my warm mouth
and he just sat there reading the newspaper.

THE PREACHER'S WIFE

She is a preacher's wife you know...
make-up on piercing green eyes
that spark at anyone
even men...
a cultured crown of hair
that looks like smeared butter...
and the way she wears clothes--
they say she writes poetry
and sends it to dirty magazines.

AND FLOWERED HATS

and powdered faces
under flowered hats
look toward tanned and balding heads
for protection against them--
black ones peeping from behind.
Lord, they mustn't come inside. . .
the smell-- Lord, I know
I've had to go out and leave
the air-conditioned house
just to pay off hands.
Smile, powdered face
Smile, and listen to
"Go ye into all the world"
and pass the plate for missions
for Africa
where
another door
is also
slamming.

OLD BLACK MAMA
LIVED IN A SHOE

We move like puppets
in so many old shoes
I can't breathe, mama
won't you
turn on the lights
and make us some bread?

Hush, child
all God's chilens'
done whitewashed the windows

MAGNOLIA POETRY

I did not write
my magnolia poem today
but drove instead
through the summer streets
of ghetto Memphis
and watched small
Black figures shift positions on the asphalt
making way for the shiny car
and the Magnolia Lady
come to get somebody's mamma
to cook her cornbread

waiting

waiting

A GIFT FROM SHIRLEY

Tree ornament eyes glowed
as Shirley
wearing the spirit of Christmas
like a warm jacket
to cover her tattered sweater
placed the can of corn and the Irish potato
bought with food stamps
into the glittering basket for the homeless
where other children have put food
from warm homes with full tables
--where Christmas melodies
stretch into the silent night.

WHO'LL TAKE CARE OF THE APPLE TREE?

Morning explodes in shifting patterns --
Taut telephone poles kilter against the landscape.
He is always up at that hour
coughing
checking the weather
mentally defining the day's work
in slow coffee gulps.
Yesterday's routine mirrors tomorrow's dilemma --
the season's calendar
once measured in neat, freshly-turned rows
now grows cluttered
with checkbook balances and loan notes;
stock markets and foreign policy
dull the harvest ritual;
man-made circumstances are more foreboding
than storms his fathers knew.
When night falls with the same glowing splendor
as has fallen for generations,
he slides under covers of his heirloom patchwork --
there is more to dream about than weather;
the peace once typical of rural life
hangs in jeopardy. . .
one more endangered American species
lies awake waiting for the dawn.

SOLD

SUMMER DREAMS OF RIVER MORNINGS

My mind flicks
with the fire on the waves
with the breeze against black grass
to a tale told by the cottonwood--
how last night's crickets
were shocked at the firecrackers
like miniature space crafts exploding
in surprise and surrender
the driftwood
with the meaning of trees
all but bleached from its memory
came alive in the morning sun
and in the long lazy walks in the sand
and the driftwood and summer morning secrets
whispered only to me
that lovely summer
I learned the meaning of rivers
and wrote it
over and over in the sand

TO MY SON ON THE SUBJECT OF WHEELS

OR THE VALUE OF HANGING OUT ANY WINDOW ON ANY SUNNY AFTERNOON
for Guy Jr.

"Just driving around"
you say
with no destination
but requesting the family Ford
moving I wonder how fast
in that no direction
like almost any other mother's 17-year-old son
blazing curls the envy of any daughter
jeans patched loud enough
to keep beat with
heavy percussion music
which you accompany on your own trumpet
crying out
"Me, too."
"Me, too, what?" we both wonder--
Yet, you with mind and imagination
quick to snatch almost anything
like almost, but not quite, any other mother's son--
it is I who wonder as you pull out
if you will ever find
that there is more to driving
than making wheels go round.

"SEE HOW THEY RUN"

Into the spiral of life every
lace-tossed moment spins... *"cut off their tails
with a carving knife..."* Just to
"see how they run.."
My mother gave me her mink coat
but I can't wear it around my good friends
because Eleanor pickets the fur stores.
My wool coat has no mink-eyed ghosts sewn in,
but I like wearing the mink anyway.
My son, Charlie, had a beloved pit bull.
Spot climbed over the fence one day when
Charlie left town without him.
We drove the neighborhood... for hours...for days...
posted rewards...went to the pound--
then Charlie came home
and nobody said a word about pit bull fights
or experimenting on animals--
but Charlie cried anyway.
The woman in Woolworth's would not buy
her angelic daughter a pink baby chicken.
The father told his wife not to worry
about baby chickens when petty dictators
could blacken the waters with deadly crude
and blood from children planted among war targets...
But the little girl cried anyway.
"Did you ever see such a sight in your life?"

43

ECHOES FROM ANOTHER THUNDER

I took my grandmother shopping
white-haired
fragile...
once so robust
and held her trembling arm
to keep her from falling...
she used to hold mine.

"I want to go home with Grandma"
had been my constant childish plea.
She gave of herself
singing songs
reading stories
and holding me close
when the thunder came.
At her house she made me feel special...
now her visit with me
plagued by arthritis
and a weak heart...
We all laughed at the circus clown--
my grandma,
my grandson and I--
just as when she took me long ago.

44

Taking her back to the nursing home,
"I enjoyed my visit,"
Grandma echoes
my childish goodbyes of long ago.

I do not mind when she repeats her story
nor do I mind the slowness of her walker;
but when the door closes
on her tiny gray cubicle,
a discordant chord clangs
and I am a child
alone in the thunder.

WIND SONG FROM ANOTHER MIDNIGHT

The wind sighs a little
just a little
   to echo her breath
as she steals from the silence
   of once was
      will be
   never can. . .
and night
      so soft
   the wind cries
   gently. . .
      he is there
      yet beyond
   the boundary
that final certain boundary
she is not quite ready to cross.
How empty midnight memories hang
   in that quaint half-world
until that moment when she
   releases her breath
         to
   dream again. . .

46

A CUP OF LIFE

To taste of death
is to see the ashes of earth.
If the heart of man
can believe in the soul
of a whispering tree
how much less
can he see the body
as a wounded crucible of flesh
broken pottery returning
to the womb of dust.
Does the weary traveler think
the cup from which he drinks
will one day be broken?
Nor does water cease to exist
because it enters
the body of man.
Each life is a cup of water--
the body returns to dust
but the water remains
living within the memory
of all the lives it touched.
How much less a miracle
that man should live again
when there is life
in each drop of rain

MIDNIGHT SKY

I lingered at your bed one winter night.
The room was white as angels in the snow--
A shadow fell across our love's delight--
Your face was swollen, but I loved you so.

Your pain
was my pain--
I cried
within.

Those miles of tubes that bound you to this life
Held promises of laughter yet to come.
I searched for stars across the midnight sky. . .
I lingered at your bed one winter night.

OBSERVATIONS FROM UNDER THE BED

I lie
under the bed
warmed by exploding prisms
drafted from your pen.
The night is alive
with golden dancers...
green delights...
the day is shrouded
in comings and goings
and the times you pulled me
from under the bed to explore
my yellow eyes and run your fingers
through velvet fur
amused at my felicitous purring
for another saucer of cream.

BETWEEN THE BLADES
OF LIFE I am severed veins
in confusion
startling a brain that could not
keep pace with the stinging wound

when

no reason
one day I find a button from his
shirt in my apron pocket
and
the lost earring he
bought me
at Overton Square

before I knew it
my finger stung from the knife
that slipped

blood spilled against a
jelly stain on the counter

stone
between razor and knife
is image honed
finely-chiseled
day by day
then
one day

I look in the mirror
and know scars have dignity--
and I am more
than blood and stone.

50

SUNSET

For Kenneth Lawrence Beaudoin,
who now is blind,
named Poet Laureate of the River
by the Poetry Society of Tennessee

Sunrise/sunset--the same now
as night settles in to stay.
The poet has found no words
that will say
how the lost sunrise still lingers in his mind
with a pastel sunset from a distant dream.
"Sunrises are more beautiful,"
he used to say,
"in Mississippi County, Arkansas
and coming up over the Mississippi River."
The sun wakes up fertile delta farmland
with jewels across a dazzling scape.
Mirrored in dark waters,
gold and pastel lights
paint images
creative tongues have sought to sing
since the first Red man called to the
father of waters.
The morning seems so far away
that will end the daily night
and begin
the unending sunrise
when the poet will find the words.

51

MISSISSIPPI RIVER LOVE BALLAD

Once I loved a river man--
he worked the barge for weeks
came home limp
all life sweated from his body
cursing
yet he always returned to the river
his merciless mistress.

Geography books lie!
The source of the Father of Waters
is not in Minnesota
nor does it end in the Gulf of Mexico.
Its source is blood
and delta soil
in waters painted more
with black earth than
of blue sky
and though the sun pulls its waters
to the sky
and the wind
takes them to the sea
the river never ends
but remains throughout thousands of years.

I can imagine pagan rituals
when ancient tribesmen
threw virgins into
swollen waters
and I see more blood on the
limp bodies of Black men
hurled into
the river by clansmen
a matter which really
had nothing to do with the river.
I see a lonely man
and a girl of sixteen
jumping together
from the Tennessee-Arkansas bridge
to see if the river cares.
And two little girls wading along a sandbar
are snatched
in one whimsical moment when laughter
is lost in yesterday's sand castles.
But then when the sun or the moon
makes dark waters beautiful
with hints of power beneath
and the cottonwood and the pine
tell the same story
as the wind on the waves
I remember my river man--
he left me long ago
but he always returned
to the river. . .

THE DUMB SUPPER

"A Dumb Supper" from the days when silence was silly is one of the things old timers talk about when they gather on the Sunday after Memorial Day for their annual pot luck dinner in the Whitton Baptist Church near the old Whitton Cemetery where their ancestors lie .

It has been 50 or 60 years since the last dumb supper--so called because nobody was supposed to talk--but was only yesterday in the memories of some.

Mrs. Frank Dean and Mrs. Gladys Bullard recalled the old custom. Their mothers were twin sisters, Mrs. Mary Eulalia Trexler Gary and Mrs. Sarah Australia Trexler Mooring, who were pioneers of Mississippi County.

One dumb supper especially stands out in Mrs. Bullard's memory. It was given by her young cousin Julia Mooring, now Mrs. Dean, and she even remembers the trip to the hostess' home.

"The mule's hooves couldn't have made more noise on the cobblestones of Memphis than on those beaten cow paths. Some parts of the thicket were very dark because of the vines and possum grapes interwoven with the black haw, pecan, wild plum, cottonwood, dogwood, sycamore, hog apple and oak trees which covered the area up to the Mississippi River. We always watched for sweet gum, even though we would have to chew rags to clean the sticky mess from our teeth."

Mrs. Dean's memory is just as good:

"Mother tried to have everything ready when the girls arrived on horses or mules in wagons. If we could serve and eat the whole meal without saying a word, we would see our future husbands.

"We did everything by motions. I can just see Addie Proffit pinching in the air, and her twin sister Rado giving her the salt. Someone else pretended to be crying to get the onions.

"They like to have never guessed what I wanted when I kept beating on the table. I just wanted beets. Ethel Day would flap her arms for chicken. The funniest thing was the way one of the girls rolled her eyes around for the black-eyed peas.

"But with all our motioning and carrying on my older sister Kate would get anything she wanted by just pointing at it. "She was grown and we were all around 16 or so. But my brother Johnny, who was 13, made faces and snickered when Mother wasn't looking, and it was terrible not to be able to tell on him."

"It was Kate who slipped out and rounded up all the boys as a joke. At the end of the supper they came and stood by our chairs. We nearly fell out laughing just like young folks today would do at something unexpected like that."

After supper the young people went outside for dancing to such old songs as "Jump Josie":

Four in the ring and they can't jump Josie,
Four in the ring and they can't jump Josie,
Four in the ring and they can't jump Josie,
How I love Miss Susie Brown.

The girls were awakened the next morning by shots from a pea shooter. It turned out that young Johnny Mooring--Mrs.

Dean's brother--was the culprit but the girls weren't sure then and used the incident as an excuse to start a pillow fight.

By the time the pillow fight was settled, the girls noticed some of their whale-bone corsets were missing. They finally retrieved them with a fishing pole from a big hog apple tree nearby.

Mrs. Dean remembers the dress she was planning to wear to church the next day.

"It was a store-bought muslin dress with a white bertha and a straw hat with blue streamers. My stockings were white with black butterflies. I was so proud of it the first time I wore it. I tried so hard to keep it clean. We rode the wagon all the way to Frenchman's Bayou (a settlement on the Mississippi River) six miles away. We went to church and to a dinner on the ground, but I ended up sitting on a piece of jelly cake for all my pains."

Next to admiring each other's clothes, the favorite pastime of the girls was telling funny stories.

One story Mrs. Bullard likes to retell concerns the Day twins and some sweet gum. The young cousins, Gladys Gary and Julia Mooring, usually attended the nearby Freewill Baptist Church where Gladys' future father-in-law, the Rev. J. H. Bullard, preached as a part of his circuit. But sometimes they went to the old Webber Methodist Church where the sermons were supposed to be extra good.

"One Sunday at the Webber Church, Mrs. Day gave her daughters two 'chaws' of sweet gum she had saved for them in her pocket book. Ethel was upset because her sister, Rosie, got the larger piece. In front of Rosie sat Miss Mattie Kerr. She had come down the Ohio River with the Whitton family as a

Dumb suppers and dinners on the ground have largely gone the way of such customs as rural singing schools such as this one at Whitton, Arkansas. Gladys Gary (lower right), recalled some of those social highlights from an earlier Arkansas to her granddaughter who wrote this story for *The Commercial Appeal*, April 20, 1970. Gladys later married a singing school chum, Pete Bullard (upper right).

housekeeper, and she was the one who had the name of the community--Dead Timber, so called because the New Madrid Earthquake of 1812 left so much dead timber--changed to Whitton in honor of the family of the doctor who made such a contribution to the community.

"Miss Mattie suffered from rheumatism, and she never stood to sing or to pray. Rosie happened to be standing with her head bowed over Miss Mattie's high coiled hair. Ethel picked up a 'Bessie Bug' crawling on the back of the pew and put it on Rosie's arm out of revenge. Rosie jerked her arm back, and her mouth flew open. The sweet gum fell in the middle of Miss Mattie's snowy coil of braids.

DINNER ON THE GROUND:
Boy in hat (center full face) is Pete Bullard--his father in white suit
(upper right) Rev. J. H. Bullard, Circuit Riding Preacher

Gladys Gary shortly before her marriage to Pete A. Bullard (right).

IN MEMORIAM

On September 1, 1968, a great man left this part of the world and took the veil of reality with him. The fact that his name is not in *Who's Who,* or in *Americana,* may have decreased the need for people to pay homage out of respect for his position but could not decrease the need for friends and family to express their love for a man who had lived almost all of his 74 years in a rural community his father helped carve out of the wilderness of the Arkansas Delta. He fought in World War I, and did his banking on the joys of life: friendship, integrity, fishing, hunting. This was an important man; he would have been important even if he were not my grandfather.

Pete and Gladys Bullard, always a unit, honoring one must include honoring the other, did accumulate a fortune on this strange earth--investing carefully and continually, receiving the dividends until that day in September when he received his half of the principle from a higher Kingdom and the woman was left to continue the legacy. She must have felt as if she were cut in two, as indeed she was, that fateful day when she took time to go back to bed so he could hold her for a few minutes. The fortune accumulated was one that cannot be bought with anything less than sincerity, love, and dedication to Christian faith and to the idea that life is what you make of it--the only fortune that can be taken past death.

So many times I would run to see Granddad's "catch" and he always had a "blue-eyed catfish" or a "blue-eyed perch" just for his blue-eyed granddaughter, which would certainly, in my childish eyes, have been caught for me and for no other. It was skinned or scaled and delivered to the other half of the unit who cooked it as only Grandmas can cook and do all the other countless acts of love only Grandmas will even want to do.

Grandma always said that flowers were for the living-- that is why this is written--out of my love for her and in appreciation of all she is and has been, as well as for Granddad who is still sitting on Mother's couch arguing politics, or delighting in his great-grandchildren, or sprawled out in front of television or radio turned to a Cardinal game, or gathering okra and tomatoes from his vegetable garden. Just maybe you could convince me he is not here if first you assure me that there is after all such a thing as blue-eyed catfish in heaven.

This was first published in Voices International in 1968 when I was editor. Grandma Gladys joined Granddad Pete twenty- four years later.

TACKER FAMILY--LEGENDS UNWRITTEN:
John, Dorothy, Tom
Joe (Frances' grandfather) Artie's mother, Arie(Brown), William
Doug, Ethel, Pat, Andy (Alfred yet to come).

Joe and Lela Pearl Tacker

Bobby (top), Frances, Dorothy, Cletus
Nancy, Linda, Janice and Cletus Jr. Tacker (1948)

FIVE GENERATIONS:
Dorothy Tacker, Frances Cowden, Gladys Bullard,   Marcelle and Masoud Zarshenas

REVIVAL

The best time of the summer--a revival in our community--lasted from 10 days to two weeks. Everyone showed up. The Baptist attended the Methodist revivals and the courtesy was returned. People from other communities came too.

When we ran out of space, some pulled up their cars and listened to the sermons through the open windows. My daddy used to stay in the car with my younger brother and sister when they were small. The car seat was much more comfortable to sleep on than the wooden benches inside.

Baptist revivals were our chance the hear the fabulous across-the-piano-playing of Mrs. Helen Forrester (I had taken lessons from her, but they didn't stick like they did with my sister, Janice). But then we had to sit through "Just As I Am," with " without one plea," many more times than at our church.

We lived just down the road from the Methodist Church, closer than anyone else, and we were the first ones there and the last ones to leave. We kept up with everyone who did, or didn't come to the revivals.

Visiting preachers, our regular preacher and their families took turns eating with the families of the congregation. Sometimes my daddy killed a goat and my mother barbecued it. They all said they liked it, though I preferred the fried chicken that most other people served. And there was plenty of home-made ice cream and more deserts than we usually had. It was even more fun if the visiting preacher had a handsome son.

Like my parents, many of the older people in our community had met and courted their future spouses at revivals. When you think of all the places young people go to meet today, it wasn't such a bad idea. Both my mother and father had relatives in Dyess. Also we shared our preacher with Dyess Methodist, so we went there often. I once met Tommy Cash, Johnny's brother, at a revival in Dyess. Johnny Cash was getting to be quite famous, though we had not yet heard of Elvis.

At each revival the visiting song leader taught special songs to the children before the sermon. It was fun learning new songs each year. One favorite, "Down in my Heart," had so many verses we thought we would never learn them. I once heard my baby sister, Linda, singing instead of "I've got the peace that passeth understanding down in my heart..." singing "I've got a piece of sandwich down in my heart."

All of the songs were wonderful, and we had the choruses memorized long before we could read, "Wash me and I shall be whiter than snow..." " We shall come rejoicing bringing in the Sheaves...." But we looked on the books anyway. My mother sometimes sang a solo; but when she sang "Amazing Grace," it sounded so good, everyone sang softer so we could hear her. The invitation was given over and over, and when we ran out of verses, we started all over again or did the chorus once last time, again and again.

The only revival I remember not enjoying was a tent meeting in Tyronza when I was about five. The evangelist was very famous for his fire and brimstone sermons. The next Sunday I tried to repent and be saved, but when I went up to the front to join the church, they laughed at me and told me to sit down. It was Communion, and not a call to be saved, that they

67

were all going to. They let me know one had to join the Church before they could take communion, and I was too young to do either. For many months I used to look up at the darkening colors of dusk in the brilliant Delta sky, afraid that I would die before I could join the Church.

The best revival was when my father joined the Church. We were all surprised because he had said that he thought that Baptist songs and sermons were better. But that night he didn't seem to mind. Everyone in church was crying, and it was the best time of the whole summer.

WHITTON ELEMENTARY

It was hard to believe that the school went to the eleventh grade when my mother attended there. There must have been several grades in each room. By the time I started school it housed only the elementary grades. Even then, once I got past the second grade, I was always in the same room with either my brother, Bobby, who was in the grade behind me or with Elaine Nunnally and Susie Minor who were in the grade above me.

It was a red brick building with five classrooms, two restrooms, a stage and an auditorium that doubled as a gym. Across the playground was a log-cabin community building that doubled as a cafeteria. A "teacherage" was the third part of the school property. It was a duplex with the principal and his wife living on one side. All of the female unmarried teachers lived on the other side--which consisted of three bedrooms opening into a common kitchen and living area. The school complex and the store across the road identified Whitton community. Even the community churches were a mile in different directions from the school.

I remember getting a whipping in the first grade when Miss Womble caught me underlining in the reading book with chalk while listening to the adventures of Dick and Jane being read by another student. The next year, my friend Jane's mother, Mrs. Sarah Chandler, started teaching first grade and became legend with her patience and understanding. This was too late for me. But later, I felt vindicated when in college I was taught to underline important parts as a memory aid. As an English teacher, I always had my own students underline important parts in their state-owned books. In that respect, I guess I got the last word in on Miss Womble.

Fortunately, my second grade teacher was also legend. Mrs. Harper Oates was a friend of my grandmother's and always made me feel special, even when I spent one sunny October recess in the room crying because I knew I would never learn to write in cursive letters. I realized later that she was one of those people who made everyone special, especially when she became my Sunday School teacher a couple of years later. Her daughter Frances, who married Gene Little, continued in her tradition and became a counselor for the Methodist Youth Fellowship. She was also a special friend to many young people.

Other teachers were also important to my future. J. D. Roberts, who was superintendent of Whitton Elementary later became principal and my teacher at Wilson High School. He made me a star in his civics and history classes. I later majored in social studies, in part, because of his influence. Also, Dennis Mullen, who was both principal and my seventh and eighth grade teacher, gave me the skills and an understanding of myself that helped me set goals for college even before I got to high school.

The summer after I graduated from the eighth grade, the old school burned, and the building that took its place for a few years was more appropriately sold for a tool shed. By then all neighborhood children, and not just the high school students, were bused to Wilson, twenty miles away as a part of the consolidation with Wilson Schools.

Although I doubt any schools now exist like Whitton Elementary, I was lucky to be influenced by three great teachers in such a small place.

Whitton Elementary School as painted by Marthilde Nunnally.
Use of the painting, courtesy of Elaine Nunnally Davis.

MARTHILDE'S GROCERY

Right across the road from Whitton Elementary School was the place to go if you had a nickel or even a penny. There were big glass jars of penny cookies. These were large cookies that would cost you from 35 to 50 cents today. There was a penny drink, a small paraffin bottle of colored drink, and a wide selection of candy that sold for a penny.

Fast food in those days was going to Marthilde's for bologna and cheese. But there were other ways to go for groceries. For many years Uncle Shorty Wages' rolling store came all the way from Truman. A forerunner of the ice cream truck of today, it was equipped with dry ice that stopped along a scheduled route. However, my uncle sold not only ice cream, but also staples, bottled drinks, and bologna, (pronounced "baloney"), not only to us, but to a large rural area. There were also Saturday visits to Tyronza or Marked Tree for the main groceries and for drinking water. Tyronza was famous for its artesian well. In a time when every home had his own pump, many produced what we called "iron water." This water had a bitter taste and turned reddish after it sat for awhile. We took empty bottles and filled them with good water.

But Marthilde's was more than a store, it was a gathering place. Since she also had a beauty shop, her store was the local newspaper. When we were in our early teens, she moved the beauty shop to her home and used the store space to put in a juke box and a drink machine. There is where we all learned to do the fifties' 'bop.'

Marthilde Nunnally's daughter, Elaine, was only a year older that I. We spent a lot of time together since we attended the same church and every other year we were in the same school room. In fact, Elaine's older sister, Shirley, not only taught us to dance but was the only one to chauffeur us to neighboring towns, until Susie Minor was allowed to drive her dad's pick-up truck. By the time we were cruising neighboring towns in Boots Minor's Chevrolet truck, the Drive Inn, featuring the dairy cone and the hamburger, was a vital part of teenage life even in our small towns.

If we did not have a date on Saturday night, we met at Marthilde's--which was also the only place to buy gas for seven or eight miles in each direction and drove from Tyronza to Marked Tree to Lepanto and back to Tyronza, which unlike the other two towns had no Drive Inn. But Tyronza's one street business area did have stopping points--two cafe hang-outs. The boys would get in their cars and follow us around to the other towns. It was in one of Tyronza cafe's that I was to meet my children's father, Guy Brinkley.

Marthilde's Grocery continued to be the center of the community long after the elementary school was sold for a tool shed and the community building and the "teacherage" had been torn down. Then the rest of the children, and not just the high students, as in our day, were bused to Wilson.

Today, Marthilde's--or Nunnally's Grocery--as the sign still reads--is just an empty building--like so many other rural landmarks. But for those few who grew up in Whitton, Arkansas, just on the southern tip of Mississippi County, it was just as important as Piggly Wiggly or even the Peabody Hotel to our contemporaries across the river in Memphis.

ODELIA

She was fascinating. Odelia was thin, and probably middle-aged, although we lumped together everybody taller than we were--old meant white hair which she didn't have. She had black braids under bright scarves.

Jane Chandler lived next door to "Shug" Banks, and Odelia lived in a tiny house across the road from him--she was his maid. He was the only one we knew personally with a maid.

Jane and I would often go home with each other from church in the morning and then go back to our respective homes after church that night. We loved to go to Odelia's house on Sunday afternoon until Jane's mother called us in for supper. We would stay with Odelia, listen to her stories and jokes and watch her cook fried chicken. I had never seen anyone put that much pepper in the flour.

"Jane-Girl, who 'dat you got with you," she would always say in her teasing voice.

"Odelia, you remember Frances." Jane would always answer.

Then Jane would ask her if she were cooking for her boy friend. And Odelia would pretend she didn't have a "man-friend." But we knew she did because Jane had seen him.

While watching her cook we would wish we could taste the fried chicken and the cornbread she put in her turnip greens, but we never could. It was all right for Jane to eat what Odelia cooked in Mr. Banks' kitchen, but we were not allowed to eat in a Black person's home.

But Odelia's home was fun. Her Sunday hats were hung on nails near her bed. The wood stove kept the two-room house warm. We always read Odelia's walls. I thought it was clever of her to paper her tiny house with newspaper and magazine pages instead of ordinary wall-paper. Over the years she added more comic strips and pictures of flowers cut from magazines. I guess she got them from "Mr. Shug," as she called Mr. Banks. Odelia's was the only home belonging to a Black person we ever had the opportunity to visit when we were children.

When Albert Banks was elected county judge, he later moved to Blytheville. But in Whitton, his large farm which contained Odelia's tiny house was next to the Black community of Birdsong. The main road stretched around in sort of a semicircle to the other Black community which was Denwood, that had its own store and cotton gin. There were many Black families who lived and worked there on Chauncy Denton's plantation.

Many years later, I was to visit Birdsong for the first time, and find a community of Black farmers most of whom owned their own small farms. There were stores, churches, a famous barbecue vendor and people with an independent and generous spirit. The children of Birdsong, as well as Denwood, whom I never met, grew up and attended high school at Wilson Trade school across the track and out of sight from the Wilson High School we attended. Odelia was our only real contact with that other world.

In later years, Jane and I have talked about how much we enjoyed knowing Odelia. Though other eyes would probably have seen it as a shack--to Jane and I--Odelia lived in a delightful playhouse.

COWS, PIGS, AND HORSES

As a farming family, we grew cotton, soy beans and some wheat for our livelihood. On the side, Daddy raised livestock for trading as well as for food. He traded so often, that the only animal we had any length of time was our jersey milk-cow. Unlike children I read about in books, I had no special animal friends; and I had nightmares about cattle. I would find myself in a pen with them with no way to climb out. None of my brothers or sisters shared my concern and often played in the pens with our cattle and pigs.

No nightmare of mine could equal the horror we faced the day the sow got Cletus Jr. My mother was ironing when we heard screams. She threw down her iron and jumped through the window--knocking out the screen as she went. When my sister and I got outside, my mother was getting my two-year-old brother away from the sow who had tasted blood. Everyone was screaming. When she got him back to the house, bloody and muddy, she cleaned him up. Mother with Daddy, who had been fetched from the field, took him to Dyess for stitches.

The only farm animals I really liked were horses. Unfortunately, the way my daddy traded, we had one occasionally, but never for long. We felt lucky to be able to ride around the pasture taking turns with our friends, led by my father. I fell off an old jenny once and she stepped on me, but I forgave her because she was a member of the horse family. Horses are beautiful, even in dreams.

The Brinkley Bunch:
Charles, Marcelle Zarshenas, Guy Jr., Clay, Saeed Zarshenas
(center) Elizabeth (Guy's wife)

ABOUT THE AUTHOR

Born Frances Anita Tacker, June 20, 1939, in Whitton, South Mississippi County, Arkansas, to Cletus and Dorothy Tacker, she has had a life-time love affair with the beauty and power of nature. The eldest of six children, she constantly sought solitude to write in her diary, to play with her watercolors, or just to look at the beauty of the flat delta countryside. She lived with her maternal grandparents, Pete and Gladys Bullard, in Whitton when she was in the first grade while the rest of the family was still in Black Oak, Arkansas. Later that year, they all moved to the family home of her paternal grandparents, Joe and Lela Tacker. Her parents still live there in a much expanded version.

Frances attended Whitton Community School through the eighth grade. Her Grandmother Gladys was one of two cooks at the cafeteria which fed the whole school consisting of five classrooms of students (After the second grade there were two grades in each room). She spent a great deal of her childhood with the Bullards who took her to many extended family gatherings where she learned to treasure her family heritage.

Frances graduated co-valedictorian from Wilson High School, Wilson, Arkansas in 1957. She attended Arkansas State and the University of Arkansas. In 1968 she received her M. S. E. in English from A.S.U. By this time, she had become involved in the world of contemporary poetry. She published poetry in a number of literary journals, many of the poems appeared in her book, *Etchings Across the Moon.* She edited *Voices International,* a *South and West* publication for the first three years it was published.

Except for a short period when she reported for *The Commercial Appeal* in Blytheville, Arkansas, Frances has been a teacher of high school English, art and social students in Arkansas, Missouri, and Tennessee--She is presently teaching art at Lester Elementary in Memphis. She has been active in the Art Teachers Association and served for two years as chairperson of that organization.

A life member of the Poetry Society of Tennessee, she has served in almost all of the organization's offices and was named Poet Laureate of P. S. T. for 1989. Many of the poems in this book have won prizes in monthly, annual, or festival contests sponsored by P. S.T.

Frances is a Letters and Art member of The National League of American Penwomen and Artists, Chickasaw Branch. She has also won awards for pottery and jewelry in Memphis Association of Craft Artists shows.

Frances' husband, Dean Cowden, who has always supported her endeavors in art and in poetry, is in the brass wholesale business and car stereo business with her three sons, Guy Jr., Charles, and Clay Brinkley. Frances and Dean are members of Colonial Park United Methodist Church where Frances sings in the choir.

Considering herself to be a "Jack of all trades and master of none," Frances hopes to change that with *GRANDMOTHER EARTH CREATIONS*. With the help of her attorney daughter, Marcelle Zarshenas, and later one or more of her grandchildren, Frances hopes to establish a publishing company that will work for the preservation of our earth so that all children and grandchildren will be able to experience its beauty.

Frances has lived in Memphis for the past 22 years. In fact, except for a short time, she has never lived far from the Mississippi River--the inspiration for this collection.

Frances and Dean Cowden